Another Psalm

Another Psalm

Poems by

Bill Schulz

© 2024 Bill Schulz. All rights reserved.
This material may not be reproduced in any form, published,
reprinted, recorded, performed, broadcast,
rewritten, or redistributed without
the explicit permission of Bill Schulz.
All such actions are strictly prohibited by law.

Cover design by Shay Culligan
Cover image by Autumn Schulz

ISBN: 978-1-63980-677-5

Kelsay Books
502 South 1040 East, A-119
American Fork, Utah 84003
Kelsaybooks.com

for Autumn, always

Acknowledgments

I am grateful to Mike Bove, Bill Burtis, Jim Crenner, Michael Hettich, Marilyn A. Johnson, Stephen Kuusisto, and Jeri Theriault for their guidance and encouragement.

And to the recovery community of Portland, Maine—I'm forever grateful for showing me the way out.

Contents

In Evergreen Cemetery	13
August Peaches	14
The Right Key	15
Pope's Grotto	16
I Don't Understand the Equator	17
Un Ombra (shadow)	26
Awake	27
Ferry Beach	28
The Nearness	29
In the Shadows	30
Angels	31
Adagietto Sehr Langsam	32
Elegies	33
New Englander	36
Notes to Martin	37
Collins Pond	39
Raised Beds	40
Adagio Non Troppo	41
I Asked a Bird	42
Nullitatis	43
By the Chama River	44
Another Psalm	45
One Bird's Feeble Song—notes to MJ	46

*You have kept count of my tossings,
put my tears in your bottle.
Are they not in your record?*

—Psalm 56

*E quindi uscimmo a riverder le stelle.
Then we came forth, to see again the stars.*

—Dante Alighieri, the last line of *The Inferno*

*I am larger, better than I thought,
I did not know I held so much goodness.*

—Walt Whitman, from *Song of The Open Road*

In Evergreen Cemetery

Mockingbirds flit
limb to stone.

A hawk whistles, high
alone. Cardinals gone.

My morning birds
gone, songs done.

Now two crows,
playing in the pines

recall the memories
of a boy—clear, clean.

August Peaches

We moved to Steiner
as peaches appeared
at the farmers' market
on Filmore where

Curtis Mayfield played
on big green
speakers
in the parking lot

near the Safeway where
someone was shot.
Those peaches
were heavy

with sweet water.
Those peaches
turned water
to wine.

The Right Key

for Michael Hettich

This bird I know
was trying to sing

each morning
in the woods

behind my house.
She never seemed

to find the right key
and this morning

she just quit. Now
the only sounds

are acorns falling
from the oak trees

we felled so many
years ago.

Pope's Grotto

Alexander Pope was 4'6"
shorter than a lilac bush.

He'd built a grotto, stone walls
covered with brilliant gems,

minerals and stalagmites
on his estate in Twickenham,

not 10 miles from Charing
Cross. Samuel Johnson said

he'd built the grotto under
the road to spend the days

in darkness shaking his fist,
cursing poets on their

way to London. I was sad
to learn Johnson's gossip

was untrue—the grotto leads to
a sunlit garden by the Thames.

I Don't Understand the Equator

See, we don't love, as flowers do,
out of a single year; where we love,
immemorial sap mounts into our arms.
                              —Rilke

I don't understand the equator,
equinox or solstice.

I know the earth is round and
the sun focuses light and warmth

on one half of the ball at a time.
But why does the earth tip?

The antipode of where I sit
is winter on the Indian Ocean.

*****

we were having lunch
with friends

in a seaside town
I fell asleep when

you talked about
art and poetry

when I woke up
they were gone

and you were gone
someone left sun

glasses and when
I tried them on

I felt like Robert
Redford

*****

A bird repeats "here, here" and
keeps moving from tree to tree.
I follow the best I can.

*****

Like shades
in a forest, mist
rising through trees,

my two daughters live
a breath away,
never speaking to me.

*****

He just realized he can't sing anymore.
So he dreams of dancing and
kisses in the parking lot.

*****

Autumn said:
    there's a man
        outside
you might
    want to meet.
        He says
there are interesting
    things going on
        in the mountains.

*****

"Alexa, coffee on."
"I guess so."

"Alexa, light on."
"Why bother? All is darkness."

*****

In the middle of the night
a fox screech or
was it a child
in pain?
Shortly after a bird
cried, "reader reader."

*****

I'm puzzled in purgatory.

*****

My sister called yesterday crying about D-Day and Normandy, where our father had been wounded by a land mine or grenade. She'd had a dream that he had been executed by firing squad and she was forced to watch.

*****

I was never a boy scout. The uniform said comply and I didn't. Though I would like to know how to sharpen a knife.

*****

I freed god from
the capital letter.

Now I am free.

******

Autumn wrote:

I met god, you,
you and my children.

I soared under the ocean,
into the cosmos, up

to mountaintops, I gave
birth and was birthed

at the same time and
felt connected to all

my female ancestors
through a chain of DNA.

How was your day?

*****

Years
passing beneath
my feet. My
eyes never
looking up.

*****

I just realized
beliefs are nothing.

There is no one true God.
There are as many gods

as there are creatures,
trees, stones, drops

of wine, planets.
I'm not sure that's

all true.

*****

I have been modifying paintings,
turning static into ecstatic.

Churches rot and fall like apples.

*****

I am on a zoom meeting. The woman sharing
said her last drink was in a Chicago bar called
The Sea of Happiness Lounge, just off
The Magnificent Mile.

*****

We were lost
driving in circles

four thousand miles
from home and

four hours south of
Milan, stopped by a

field of canola flowers,
there just for us.

*****

Sometimes I park by the house
I built by an ice pond and cry.
The birch trees she wanted
have grown, welcomed shade
I never knew.

I meant to write:
thin women running,
thin men left behind.

****

I was cutting a sweet potato with
a fine, sharp knife and thought

how easy it would be and
how difficult to clean up.

*****

My Christology professor was an old Jesuit named Don Gelpi,
a kind man with a quick intellect. I never heard anyone
call him Father Gelpi or Father Don, it was always Don.

I was in a class with five young doctoral students who were
well-trained in the head, not yet the heart. They thought
I was cute, like a mascot wearing a big clown head to class.

Don's exams were one-on-one in his office, surrounded
by hundreds, no, thousands of books. Christology is not easily
grasped. I couldn't understand this complex and complicated
Christ.

I studied for hours for the first exam. I sat in an old rocker across
from Don. He gave me a cup of tea, asking me questions,
    expecting
to have a conversation. I froze, couldn't speak.

I scared him. He brought me a glass of water.
I recovered enough to say, "It's a mystery, Don."

*****

When I learned to love the world:
August 1961. Twilight on
Babbidge Road off Blackstrap
in the back seat (black leather)
of my father's Galaxy 500
convertible. Belafonte
at Carnegie Hall
on the radio.

Sad to say
I'm on my way . . .

*****

Note to my self:
I've heard nothing from you in weeks.
Please send a word or two when you can.

*****

Though freed by handcuffs
after all those years
of hurt and hurting,

there's not a song,
kiss, or soft hand
would soothe me today.

*****

Note to Autumn:
When I go,
leave the door closed
as long as you can.
Give my soul time
to gather what
we'll need.

Un Ombra (shadow)

Un ombra in Venice is a quick shot of wine.
You have a choice to make, espresso or

un ombra, served from a window near
the Arsenale. We chose ombra, of course,

a quick kick to the back of the throat
and strolled to Harry's Bar for Bellinis,

like Hemingway would do. We carried
the shadow on the train to Milan.

Awake

Last night I slept
an old man's sleep,

dreamt old man
dreams.

You were there and
your god it seemed.

A familiar sound,
a dusty cough,

the way you
cleared your throat

to say tomorrow
I'll move again,

alone, tomorrow.

Ferry Beach

A blue heron in a thin mist,
perfectly still, still as stone

eyes the egrets,
their ivory necks,

their slender forms,
their flight away.

The Nearness

There was this
song I heard
January 2017.

I was driving
on a Sunday
evening, I had

to pull over
in the dark
to cry for

*the nearness
of you* after
you had gone.

In the Shadows

You parked in the shadows of
the Cathedral to say good-bye
with a pale smile as I walked past.

I could have stopped to say
hello. You might have let me in
to drive to the woods where once

we made love on an old woolen
blanket. Last night I tried to recall
your body, your voice, the way

you laughed at the words soft
serve. But all I could see was
the rage in your eyes, the locked

doors, and the home we left
by the ice pond. And then, you
parked in the shadows.

Angels

I've heard of angels
on ladders who sing
with no sound,

seen angels loaf
in the shade of umbrella
palms by Ashby station.

And one red-headed angel
in Spring Harbor Hospital
who came that Christmas

warming wind and water
just to keep me safe
and off my knees.

Adagietto Sehr Langsam

One evening Gustav Mahler
went to sleep in Vienna
and woke up in New York.

Finding his way to
the 60th Street Railyard
he rode the rails west

as far as Bakersfield
and when he returned
told no one where he'd been.

Gustav turned out the lights
each Friday at sundown, then
turning them on after

Sunday evening Mass,
sat in the lamplight quietly
writing his apologies.

Elegies

For one dead fox
beside the road,

two deer in the headlights
beside a dead fawn,

accidental electrocution
like Thomas Merton,

and the woman who
slipped off a cliff by

Winslow Homer's
studio. Not for me,

I botched asphyxiation
in my garage.

***

For sugar ants
by the coffee pot

I kill each morning
with my thumb.

This spring an exterminator
came to gas carpenter ants

and sucked them up
with a shop vac.

My cat Habibi'll kill a mole
or chipmunk when he can.

I could cry at the thought
of him dying but there he sits

in the road.

***

For my mother a nurse
during the war

who kept a green army
blanket in the trunk

for picnics
on the beach.

We stopped once
at a head-on crash,

she covered a body
on the road. Then,

no matter how many
times she washed it,

blood stains remained
on the blanket folded

in the trunk.

***

For my father who
studied embalming then

joined the 4th infantry
turning 25 in England

as a first lieutenant
one month before Normandy

where he was hit with shrapnel
on the road to St. Mere Eglise.

I'm looking at a black
and white photo of him

leaning over a cadaver,
holding the head

in his two hands.

New Englander

A man shovels snow for hours
in front of a pale green house

at the end of my street,
shoveling though the storm

passed hours ago and the sun
is as warm as April.

Locals call these men and these
houses New Englanders meaning

unexceptional, simple, sturdy.
I could walk through his house

in the dark wearing a blindfold
and never bump into a wall.

I'd enter through the side door
off the driveway at night,

kitchen two steps up
cellar five steps down where

I'll take your hand in the dim
light of the boiler room

and lead you to the chalk marks
and words we once scribbled

on the concrete floor.

Notes to Martin

That time I wrote
I have no friends

to Martin my old
psychologist; it's

like they all leapt
from a freight car

in black and white
on the tracks by

a river where
we used to swim. But

let me tell you about
the furnace room

where there was real
fire and I was lost

smoke rising from
my fingertips then

all neon lights for
days and nights.

In a dark corner
a woman said I'm not

your friend. My mug
shot in the news,

nervous in gas stations, lost
in town and it's true Martin

one night I woke in a closet
my hands covered in blood.

Collins Pond

for Bob Herz

Where are you going
old one? Turn around.

Collins Pond is far away.
Why move turtle slow

across the road into
the brush and gone?

Better I'd not seen you,
another life to carry

in memory.

Raised Beds

Today
sun and wind
scraped away
the last of the snow.
They always do.

Still, I was moved seeing
the raised beds
shrouded beneath
the last of winter's
ice and gravel

like mummified saints
in a side chapel,
still smelling
of chrism oil
and lilies.

Adagio Non Troppo

Just days after you died
and I was still living, the

Brahms Serenade No. 1
in D Major playing

on a classical music station
when I went to work

like any other day,
trying to let you go

slow, but not
too much.

I Asked a Bird

I asked a bird
to forgive me.

The bird
flew away.

I gave it seed,
hung a house.

The bird
flew away.

I sang alone
by an altar,

knelt and
cried.

The bird
flew away,

low over
an ice pond.

I asked a bird
to forgive me.

Nullitatis

This morning
        I pressed my hand

to my chest,
        the tight skin

between neck
        and heart,

between peace
        and fear,

closed my eyes and
        for a moment

I was nothing.

By the Chama River

Magpie wander
erratically in winter
never far
from one another.

Not as grand
as the raven
the magpie flies
lower with joy.

Resting in
cottonwoods
they comfort
one another

with a song,
sometimes
just a whispered
c'mon c'mon

I'll race you
across the river.

Another Psalm

Thank you, God
for not being

there when
I needed you.

Thank you for
not being

the way I
thought of you.

Thank you for
the friends who

said I can't, not
you, not now, not

ever. Thank you for
helping me forget

names, places,
songs, people.

Thank you
for this emptiness,

this space
to fill.

One Bird's Feeble Song—notes to MJ

*I am circling around God, around the ancient tower,
and I have been circling for a thousand years,
and I still don't know if I am a falcon, or a storm,
or a great song.*
                         —Rilke

Yahweh, or whatever name
gods were using then,
walking, no, striding across

the empty land, alone and
lonely, about to make
the first mistake,

falling to their knees
drawing a line
separating all of creation.

A small bird appears,
a yellow bird, a finch.
Then another.

***

When gods sleep
they dream of wolves
and darkness, the Tigris

and Euphrates.

***

Near dawn a tomcat
moans. I get up
to shoosh it,

feet making
a knocking sound
on the kitchen floor.

Outside, one bird's
feeble song fails
to raise the sun.

***

I once asked a well-dressed
right reverend bishop

to bless me on my way
out the door, down the long

fearful road. Brushing hair
back from my forehead, I

closed my eyes as if in prayer.
And when I opened them,

the bishop was gone. He left me
and all God's children yearning

for one simple blessing.

***

Satan went into the garage
looking for the money you'd left me.

When I pulled in, he was upside
down, encased in ice.

He whispered, *we don't
belong here.*

***

May my grave
be opened each day

and my body dried
like a walnut.

***

I drowned
in a whiskey river

as Willie sang
on the jukebox

at the Andrews Motel
in Sparta, North Carolina

Whiskey River take my mind.
Don't let her memory torture me.

Whiskey river don't run dry,
you're all I've got, take care of me.

Stay 'til closing time
and they'll give you

fresh biscuits and gravy
just before opening

for breakfast.

***

We lived on a hill
when I was a child.

Miles away on another hill
was a drive-in movie theater.

Summer nights I'd watch
movies from my bedroom

window and imagine
the words and music.

Popeye singing I'm strong
to the finish 'cause

I eats me spinach as
darkness comes. Then

Vincent Price as The Fly
whispers Help me. Help me.

And I would, truly I would have
if I hadn't fallen asleep under my bed.

***

I've been thinking about
how I would have died
700 years ago.

Infected tooth, I'd guess,
just an infected tooth.

***

Who was the first to look up
and say the word heaven?

Heaven, they said,
that's where we'll hide.

About the Author

Bill Schulz lives in Maine, not far from the farm where his ancestors settled in 1783. He received a Master's degree from the poetry program at The University of New Hampshire in 1976 and a Master's in Theological Studies from The Franciscan School of Theology in Berkeley, CA 30 years later.

His book of poetry, *Dog or Wolf,* was published independently in July 2022. He is the founder and editor of *Hole in the Head Review.*

Find out more at:
www.holeintheheadreview.com